From Panic to Power

Essential Strategies to Thrive in High-Pressure Careers

Firoz Ahmed Makrani

(Umar)

ISBN: 978-93-6087-549-7

Price: 299.00

Published and printed by:

Shashwat Publication

Office Address: Ram das Nagar,

Bilaspur, Chhattisgarh – 495001

Phones: +91 9993608164 +91 9993603865

Email: contact.shashwatpublication@gmail.com

Website: www.shashwatpublication.com

Printed in India

Foreword

It is with great pleasure that I introduce "From Panic to Power: Essential Strategies to Thrive in High-Pressure Careers" authored by Umar Rashid Makrani. In this insightful guide, Umar offers essential strategies for navigating the pressures of high-stress work environments and transforming challenges into opportunities for personal and professional growth.

In today's fast-paced corporate world, stress has become an inevitable companion for many professionals. With clarity and expertise, Umar delves into the roots of workplace stress, from the dynamics of office politics to the psychological triggers that contribute to feelings of overwhelm. By understanding the underlying causes of stress, readers are empowered to confront and overcome insecurities, fostering a sense of empowerment and self-esteem.

What sets "From Panic to Power" apart is its holistic approach to wellness. Umar emphasizes the importance of integrating lifestyle changes for stress reduction, recognizing that true well-being encompasses physical, emotional, and organizational dimensions. Through practical strategies and actionable insights, readers learn to cultivate resilience and balance in their professional and personal lives.

Central to this book is the idea of transforming stress into success. Umar challenges readers to reframe their perspectives and embrace challenges as opportunities for growth. By adopting a mindset of resilience and adaptability, individuals can harness the power of stress to propel themselves toward greater success and fulfillment in their careers.

As readers embark on the journey outlined in "From Panic to Power," they are invited to embrace a new paradigm of empowerment and possibility. Umar's wisdom and guidance serve as a beacon of light, illuminating the path from panic to power and offering hope and inspiration to all those navigating high-pressure careers.

I am confident that "From Panic to Power" will serve as a valuable resource for professionals seeking to thrive in today's competitive and demanding work environments. May this book empower you to harness the inherent challenges of your career as stepping stones to greater success and fulfillment.

Warm regards,

Dr. Yogendra Singh Rathore

NLP Master Practitioner | Times 40 under 40 | World Book of Records Holder

Acknowledgments

Writing this book has been a journey of introspection and discovery, one that I could not have embarked upon without the support and love of many individuals who have enriched my life in various ways.

First and foremost, I want to express my deepest gratitude to my wife, Rizwana. Her unwavering support and understanding have been my anchors in all facets of my life. Her patience and wisdom have guided me through both calm and turbulent waters, and for this, I am eternally grateful.

To my children, Abdulhasib and Faizan, who bring endless joy and perspective into my life. Abdullah, your thoughtful observations have often led me to reassess my views and grow as a person. Faizan, your unconditional love and enthusiasm are my constant reminders of what truly matters in life.

I am profoundly thankful to Dr. YS Rathore and Sheikh Mohammed Al-Naqvi, whose guidance has been pivotal in transforming my perspective and approach to life and stress management. Their wisdom has been a cornerstone of my personal and professional growth.

I must also extend a special thanks to my parents, Mr Rashid Ahmed and Late Mrs Zohra, whose nurturing and teachings laid the foundation of my character and resilience. Their love and sacrifices have shaped the person I am today.

Additionally, I appreciate those who have contributed to my understanding of stress—ironically, through the stress they brought into my life. These experiences have been invaluable, teaching me resilience and the true meaning of overcoming challenges.

This book is also a tribute to everyone who has ever faced stress and struggled to find their footing in the chaos it can bring. Your stories and experiences have inspired me to find solutions that not only help myself but may also lighten the load for others.

A special acknowledgment goes to my Guide, Mr. Samir Ranjan, whose leadership and support have significantly contributed to my professional journey. His guidance and confidence in my abilities have been great motivators for me.

Finally, I extend my gratitude to all my friends and mentors, whose advice and support have been instrumental in shaping the insights shared in this book. Your wisdom and encouragement have been my guiding lights.

From Panic to Power:
Essential Strategies to Thrive in High-Pressure Careers

Contents

Introduction: The Journey from Stress to Empowerment

Have you ever felt like your career is a constant uphill battle, where every step forward seemed to push you two steps back? You're not alone. I've been there, battling through the maze of office politics, where ambition often felt like a double-edged sword. But what if I told you that there's a way to transform this stress into a stepping stone for success?

I know how overwhelming it can feel. Early in my career, I saw the corporate world as a battlefield, where only the fiercest competitors could thrive. I was determined to rise quickly, outsmarting and outmaneuvering everyone around me. However, this approach came with unintended consequences. My relationships suffered, and my professional life became more about surviving daily battles than about real growth.

Perhaps our experiences aren't so different. Maybe you've felt the sting of competitive tension, the isolation that comes from being misunderstood, or the frustration of unrecognized efforts. This book is a reflection of not just my journey but potentially yours as well.

"**From Panic to Power: Essential Strategies to Thrive in High-Pressure Careers**" is more than just a book. It's a pathway to understanding and navigating the complexities of workplace dynamics. It's about finding balance between ambition and cooperation, and turning stressful encounters into opportunities for personal and professional development.

Through the chapters, we explore practical strategies to foster healthy relationships at work, engage effectively with colleagues, and build a reputation based on competence and mutual respect. From real-life examples to actionable advice, the book offers a blueprint for anyone looking to thrive in their career without succumbing to the pressures that often lead to burnout.

Join me on this transformative journey as we delve into the art of turning workplace challenges into platforms for growth and success. Let's redefine what it means to be successful in the corporate world, turning stress into a catalyst for achievement and fulfillment. Let's not just survive the game of office politics—let's change the game entirely.

Chapter 1

Understanding Office Politics and Ambition: The Roots of Work Stress

In the early days of my career, the corporate landscape appeared as a battleground where only the sharpest and quickest climbers could survive. Fresh out of college, armed with ambition and a drive to rise swiftly through the ranks, I stepped into this world eager to make my mark. Raised in an environment where competition was the norm, I approached my job with a mindset that everyone around me was a potential rival. My ultimate goals were clear: secure promotions and escalate my salary.

I was always on the move, working tirelessly to outshine others and prove my worth. My efforts were not just about meeting the expectations of my role; I was also keen to display my intelligence and capability directly to those at the top. Sometimes, I would bypass my direct supervisor, believing that taking my ideas straight to senior management would demonstrate initiative and bold thinking.

However, this strategy had unintended consequences. Instead of earning accolades, I began to sense a shift in how I was perceived. My boss, feeling undermined, became less inclined to mentor me or advocate for my contributions. Senior managers, too, started seeing me as overly ambitious, concerned more with my own advancement than with the collective goals of the company.

Meanwhile, my colleagues, wary of my intentions, began to guard key information, which in turn made my job increasingly difficult. The workplace I had envisioned as a ladder to success began to feel more like a maze, complicated by mistrust and miscommunication.

It was during a particularly challenging project, hampered by lack of cooperation and missing information, that I began to question my approach. Why was I alienated in a space I wanted to excel in? Was my competitive drive misdirected? These questions nagged at me, prompting a period of introspection and a reevaluation of my strategy.

This personal journey through the complex dynamics of office politics led me to understand that ambition, while a powerful motivator, needs to be tempered with an awareness of how one fits within the broader ecosystem of an organization. The realization dawned on me that the corporate world, much like the natural world, thrives on interdependence rather than isolated pursuits.

From this reflection, I learned that success in one's career is as much about fostering good relationships and engaging in teamwork as it is about individual achievement. The balance between personal ambition and collaborative contribution became my new focus, reshaping my career and my relationships at work.

As we delve deeper into the nuances of office politics throughout this book, we'll explore strategies to navigate these waters effectively. We'll discuss how to maintain integrity while being strategically aware, how to foster healthy relationships with colleagues and superiors, and how to build a reputation that is based on respect and competence, not just ambition.

As I continued to reflect on my earlier actions and the resulting isolation, I began to consider the viewpoints of my colleagues—the very individuals I had previously seen only as hurdles to my career progress. This shift in perspective was not immediate but grew from a dawning realization of the broader implications of my actions.

Empathy, the ability to understand and share the feelings of another, gradually became a tool I realized I had sorely neglected. During my rise through the corporate ranks, my focus had been sharply tuned to out manoeuvring others, securing that next promotion, to making sure my salary reflected my ambitions. However, this singular focus on personal gain had blinded me to the collaborative nature of success in any workplace. Each colleague carried their own set of ambitions, fears, and challenges, each trying to navigate through their professional landscapes as best they could.

For instance, consider Sarah, a seasoned project manager whose wealth of experience has often been a guiding light on complex projects. By sidestepping her in my earlier strategies, I had inadvertently signalled a lack of respect for her role and insights, possibly making her feel undervalued or threatened. This realization struck me particularly hard. It wasn't just about the discomfort I had caused; it was about the potential collaborative success we had missed out on because of my approach.

And then there was Mark, whose collaborative spirit I had often overlooked. His method of building consensus and sharing credit might have seemed slower or less aggressive than my own, but it had earned him the genuine respect and support of his team. Could his approach have mitigated some of the challenges I faced? Likely so.

These reflections led me to a broader understanding of the ecosystem of our workplace. A successful career is not solely the product of individual achievements but the result of interactions, relationships, and the collective efforts of many. Recognizing this was the first step in transforming my approach from one of mere competition to one of contribution and cooperation.

This journey of understanding and adjusting my approach to office politics was just beginning. I knew that to truly change the dynamics around me, I needed to dive deeper into the strategies for fostering empathy and collaboration. The following chapters will explore these strategies, examining how we can all cultivate a more empathetic and supportive workplace environment.

We will look at practical tools for developing emotional intelligence, techniques for effective communication, and the steps we can take to build a workplace where everyone feels valued and empowered. This exploration is not just about reducing workplace stress—it's about creating a foundation for lasting professional relationships and success. As we will travel along in this book, I am going to share the transition I have achieved after 25 years of my career.

Navigating Ambitions: Fostering Health in Competition

As I reflect on the earlier years of my career, where the fervor to advance and be recognized often clouded my judgment, I've come to appreciate a fundamental truth about workplace dynamics: competition, while a natural and even healthy aspect of any professional environment, must be navigated with care and awareness.

Healthy competition can spur innovation, drive individuals to exceed their limits, and push the entire team towards greater achievements. However, when the competitive spirit overshadows collaborative values, it can create setbacks not just for individuals but for entire teams. The challenge, therefore, lies in balancing our ambitions with an understanding that just as we aspire to grow and succeed, so too do our colleagues.

The Dual Nature of Ambition

Ambition is like a fire; properly managed, it can illuminate and warm, driving us forward and lighting our way through challenges. Mismanaged, however, it can consume us and those around us, leaving destruction in its wake. In the competitive cauldron of office politics, understanding this dual nature of ambition is crucial.

In my own journey, this understanding came gradually. I began to see that my relentless pursuit of advancement was not just affecting my relationships but also my overall effectiveness. Projects suffered not because of a lack of effort or dedication, but because the necessary cooperation was hindered by the competitive barriers I had erected.

Understanding Others' Ambitions

Realizing that every colleague has their own set of ambitions was a pivotal moment. Sarah, the project manager whose experience I had once undervalued, was aiming for recognition of her skills and perhaps a move into upper management. Mark, always the team player, sought to foster an environment where his leadership skills could shine through collective success. Recognizing these ambitions, I could see that our goals did not necessarily conflict; indeed, they could be synergistic if approached correctly.

Strategies for Healthy Competition

1. **Empathy and Active Listening**: One of the first strategies I adopted was to actively listen to my colleagues—not just to respond or to defend my own ideas but to truly understand their perspectives and goals. This practice not only helped in easing tensions but also opened up avenues for collaborative success that I had previously overlooked.
2. **Transparent Communication**: I learned the importance of being transparent about my ambitions and the reasoning behind my decisions. This transparency helped demystify my actions and intentions to my colleagues, paving the way for mutual trust and respect.

3. **Celebrating Others' Successes**: Instead of viewing colleagues' successes as a threat or a setback to my own goals, I began to celebrate them. This shift not only improved relationships but also created a more positive work environment, encouraging others to reciprocate.
4. **Mentorship and Shared Learning**: By engaging in mentorship and shared learning experiences, we could all grow together. I took it upon myself to both seek mentorship and offer it, facilitating an atmosphere where knowledge and skills were freely shared, reducing the zero-sum game mentality.
5. **Negotiation and Compromise**: Recognizing that not all conflicts of ambition can be directly aligned, I honed my skills in negotiation and compromise. This was particularly crucial in scenarios where project roles or leadership positions were at stake.

The Outcome of Nurturing Ambition Wisely

By integrating these strategies, the workplace transformed from a battleground of competing individual goals into a collaborative ecosystem where each person's ambitions were acknowledged and nurtured. Projects began to run smoother, and the overall stress that had once seemed an unavoidable part of the job began to diminish.

In retrospect, the understanding and adjustments I made in navigating my own and others' ambitions were not just about alleviating stress or avoiding setbacks; they were about building a foundation for long-term success and fulfillment in my career. This realization is what I hope to impart to others: that by fostering a healthy balance between competition and collaboration, we not only enhance our professional journeys but also contribute to a more dynamic and supportive work environment.

This exploration helps underline the importance of managing personal ambitions in a way that contributes positively to the workplace, ensuring that while we strive for personal success, we also uplift those around us.

As we explore the complexities of office politics and the balance between personal ambition and collective success, it's important to pause and reflect on our own experiences. The following questions are designed to help you delve deeper into your professional interactions and consider new perspectives that may enhance both your career and your relationships at work:

- Reflect on a time when your ambition pushed you to act aggressively at work. How did it affect your relationships with your colleagues? Looking back, how could you have approached the situation differently to foster a more collaborative environment?
- Think about a colleague who often seems challenging to work with. What might be their underlying motivations and fears? How can understanding their perspective change the way you interact with them?
- Recall a project where collaboration led to a better outcome than if you had pursued your own agenda. What did this experience teach you about the value of teamwork over individual competition?"

As we navigate the intricate dance of ambition and collaboration within the workplace, it becomes clear that our approach to relationships and power dynamics can significantly influence our professional trajectory and personal fulfillment. The wisdom shared by thought leaders across various fields echoes the importance of empathy, strategic thinking, and collective effort in achieving lasting success. Consider the following insights that highlight the profound impact of cooperation, empathetic leadership, and understanding the unique paths of others in our professional environments:

"It is through cooperation, rather than conflict, that your greatest successes will be derived." — Ralph Charell

"Leadership is not about being in charge. It is about taking care of those in your charge." — Simon Sinek

"Whenever you feel like criticizing any one...just remember that all the people in this world haven't had the advantages that you've had." — F. Scott Fitzgerald

"Political skill is the ability to understand others at work and to use such knowledge to influence others to act in ways that enhance one's personal and/or organizational objectives." — Gerald R. Ferris

"Alone we can do so little; together we can do so much." — Helen Keller

As we wrap up our exploration of office politics and the delicate balance of ambition, let's reflect on the core lessons learned and how they can guide us in our daily professional interactions.

1. **Balanced Ambition**: Navigating office politics successfully requires balancing personal ambitions with the broader goals of the organization. This balance fosters a healthy, cooperative workplace.

2. **Empathetic Leadership**: Embracing empathy and understanding the motivations and challenges of colleagues can transform competitive environments into collaborative ones.
3. **Strategic Interactions**: Developing political skill isn't about manipulation; it's about strategically interacting within your work environment to benefit both personal and organizational objectives.
4. **Collective Success**: Remember, the most sustainable form of success in any workplace comes from efforts that uplift the entire team, not just the individual.

As we close this chapter on the dynamics of office politics and the foundational importance of managing ambition constructively, we turn our focus to a closely related and equally critical topic: the underlying psychological factors that contribute to stress in professional settings. In the next chapter, **"The Psychology of Stress: Causes and Triggers in the Workplace,"** we will delve into the common stressors that professionals face, such as deadline pressures, insufficient information, and issues stemming from poor task delegation. Understanding these triggers will equip us with better strategies to manage and mitigate stress, enhancing not only our efficiency but also our well-being at work.

Chapter 2

The Psychology of Stress: Causes and Triggers in the Workplace

Our reactions to stress aren't just personal; they're also shaped by the wider society and the upbringing we receive. From an early age, societal norms and parental expectations can instill in us certain ways of handling pressure. For instance, if we grow up seeing adults consistently respond to stress with anxiety or avoidance, we might naturally adopt these responses ourselves. Similarly, societal pressures to succeed, exemplified by phrases like "no pain, no gain," can lead us to believe that stress is an unavoidable and even necessary part of achievement. Recognizing these deep-seated influences can be the first step toward developing healthier, more constructive approaches to managing stress. By questioning and adjusting these learned behaviors, we can set new standards for ourselves and future generations, promoting well-being as a priority both at home and in the workplace.

Stress at work is very common. While a little bit of stress can help us do our best, too much stress can make it hard to think clearly and feel good. This chapter will help us understand why certain things at work make us feel stressed. We will look at common reasons for stress like tight deadlines, not having enough information, feeling unsure of ourselves, and not being clear about what our jobs require.

We will explore how these things can make us anxious and what we can do about it. By understanding what causes our stress, we can start to make changes that help us feel less overwhelmed and more in control.

Let's take a closer look at how stress works and learn ways to handle it better, so we can work happily and more effectively.

Stress isn't just a feeling—it starts in our brains. When we face a challenging situation, such as a tight deadline or a complex project at work, our brain reacts in a way that has been shaped over thousands of years. This reaction was originally designed to help humans react quickly to life-threatening situations. Today, the same response kicks in during work-related challenges, even though they are not life-threatening.

When we face tough situations at work, like a looming deadline or a challenging task, our bodies react in a way that goes back to ancient times. This reaction is known as the fight-or-flight response, and it prepares us to either face the problem head-on or to run away from it.

Understanding Fight-or-Flight

This response starts when we feel threatened. At work, these threats aren't like the physical dangers our ancestors faced, but our body reacts in a similar way. This might happen when we worry about meeting a deadline, handling a tough project, or even fearing we might lose our job.

What Happens in Our Body

When fight-or-flight kicks in, several things happen in our body quickly:

- **Heart Beats Faster**: This helps send more blood to our muscles, getting us ready to act fast.
- **Breathing Quickens**: Our lungs work faster to get more oxygen into our blood.
- **Muscles Tighten**: Our muscles get ready to move quickly, either to tackle the problem or to escape it.
- **Senses Sharpen**: We become more alert and aware of our surroundings, ready to handle the situation.

Mental Changes

Our mind also changes its focus:

- **Focus Narrows**: We pay more attention to the threat, which can help us deal with it quickly. However, this might make it hard to see other options or solutions.
- **Other Functions Slow Down**: Our body slows down things that are not essential at that moment, like digestion, because it's using all its resources to deal with the threat.

Fight-or-Flight at Work

In the modern workplace, this response can be helpful at times, giving us the burst of energy we need to finish tasks quickly. But if we're always stressed and always in fight-or-flight mode, it can wear us down and make us less effective.

How to Manage This Response

It's important to know how to calm this response:

- **Deep Breathing**: Taking slow, deep breaths can help calm our body and mind.
- **Mindfulness**: Staying present and focused can reduce stress.
- **Planning and Problem-Solving**: Structured approaches to solving problems can prevent unnecessary stress and panic.

Understanding how to control the fight-or-flight response can help us handle stressful situations at work without getting overwhelmed. By learning to manage our body's reactions, we can stay calm and effective, even under pressure.

Enhancing Stress Management Through Structured Planning

While deep breathing and mindfulness are essential tools for managing immediate stress responses, adopting a structured approach to planning and problem-solving addresses the root causes of stress, preventing it from escalating in the first place. This proactive strategy not only helps in managing current stress but also equips us to handle future challenges with greater ease and confidence. Let's delve deeper into how structured planning and problem-solving can be implemented effectively in our daily work routines to minimize stress and enhance our productivity.

Effective Planning and Problem-Solving to Reduce Stress

When faced with daunting tasks or tight deadlines at work, stress can quickly escalate, triggering our fight-or-flight response. However, adopting a structured approach to planning and problem-solving can significantly reduce this stress, ensuring that we remain calm and effective in our roles.

Step-by-Step Guide to Structured Problem-Solving

1. **Define the Problem Clearly**: Before you can find a solution, you need to understand exactly what the problem is. Take the time to define the problem in specific terms. For instance, instead of thinking "I'm overwhelmed by work," identify the specific issue: "I need to create a detailed report by the end of the week and I don't have the necessary data."
2. **Break It Down**: Large problems can seem overwhelming, so break them down into smaller, more manageable parts. If you need to create a report, your first step might be gathering the necessary data, followed by drafting each section of the report.
3. **Set Clear Objectives**: For each part of the problem, set clear, achievable objectives. Using our example, a clear objective might be: "By Tuesday, collect all required data on sales performance from the finance department."
4. **Prioritize Tasks**: Arrange tasks in order of importance and urgency. Tackle the tasks that are most critical to solving the problem first. This not only ensures that you're focusing your efforts efficiently but also helps in managing time better.

5. **Develop a Timeline**: Create a timeline for completing tasks. A timeline acts as a roadmap, helping you see how tasks fit together and when each task needs to be completed. For the report, you might allocate one day for data collection, two days for writing, and one day for review and revisions.
6. **Use Tools and Resources**: Utilize available tools and resources to help you manage and solve problems. This could include software for project management, templates for reporting, or even consulting with a colleague who has expertise in the area you're working on.
7. **Monitor Progress**: Regularly check your progress against the timeline and objectives you've set. Adjust your plan as necessary if you find you're falling behind or if unforeseen issues arise.
8. **Reflect and Learn**: Once the task is completed, take some time to reflect on what went well and what could be improved. This reflection will enhance your problem-solving skills for future challenges.

Implementing These Steps in Daily Work

Incorporating these structured problem-solving steps into your daily work can transform how you handle stress. It turns chaotic situations into a series of manageable tasks, reduces uncertainty, and increases your control over outcomes. By planning ahead and solving problems methodically, you can prevent the panic associated with last-minute rushes and unexpected complications.

This approach not only alleviates stress but also boosts your confidence and competence in handling workplace challenges. It demonstrates to colleagues and supervisors that you are a proactive and effective problem-solver, capable of managing complex situations with ease.

Concluding Thoughts on the Foundations of Workplace Stress

As we conclude our initial exploration into how our brains react to stress, it's important to reflect on how these insights mirror our own experiences in the workplace. By understanding the physiological and psychological foundations of stress, we are better equipped to recognize the early signs and take proactive steps to manage our reactions. Each one of us has faced moments when the pressure seemed overwhelming, yet with the right tools and knowledge, we can navigate these challenges more effectively. As we move forward, let's delve deeper into the specific triggers of workplace stress. Recognizing these triggers is the first step toward creating a more supportive and resilient work environment for ourselves and our colleagues. Let's explore how common workplace situations like deadline pressures, insufficient information, and unclear responsibilities can significantly impact our stress levels and what we can do about them.

Understanding Common Triggers of Workplace Stress

Every day, we step into our workplaces carrying not just our laptops and coffee mugs but also a silent anticipation of what the day might hold for us. Whether it's the rush to meet a looming deadline, the struggle to gather essential information for a project, or the challenge of managing tasks that seem poorly defined, these situations are common stress triggers that many of us face. It's not just about the tasks themselves but how they make us feel—overwhelmed, underprepared, or uncertain. In this section, we will explore these common triggers of workplace stress. By understanding what specifically stresses us out and why, we can begin to take steps toward not just enduring these challenges, but mastering them, turning our workdays from sources of stress into opportunities for growth and satisfaction.

Deadline Pressures: Navigating Time and Stress in the Workplace

Imagine you're Emily, a graphic designer with a flair for creativity. It's Monday morning, and you've just been handed a project that requires three weeks of work. However, the deadline given is by the end of the week. Your heart sinks as you humorously wonder if your boss secretly owns a time machine they forgot to mention.

This is a common scenario in workplaces across the globe, where tight deadlines threaten not only the quality of our output but our overall well-being.

The Stress of Tight Deadlines

For Emily, and many like her, the immediate rush of anxiety about how to complete the task on time is palpable. This anxiety isn't just about meeting the deadline—it's also about fearing the consequences of not meeting it. Such deadline pressures can lead to a fight-or-flight response, causing not only mental stress but also physical symptoms like headaches and sleep disturbances. The creative thinking needed for her graphic design projects is compromised as stress narrows her focus, limiting her ability to see innovative solutions.

Moreover, this constant race against the clock can erode work-life balance, affecting both personal satisfaction and team morale. It's a cycle that's all too familiar in today's high-speed professional environments.

Tips for Managing Time Effectively

To navigate these waters without burning out, effective time management strategies are crucial. Here's how Emily might manage her project deadline with less stress:

1. **Prioritize Tasks**: Emily begins by listing out all the components of the project. She identifies the critical elements that need immediate attention and separates less urgent tasks that can wait or be delegated.
2. **Break Projects into Smaller Tasks**: By dividing the large project into smaller, more manageable tasks, Emily can tackle the project step by step. This approach makes her workload seem more achievable and less overwhelming.
3. **Set Realistic Deadlines**: Understanding her own pace and workflow, Emily communicates with her supervisor about the realistic timelines for a project of this scale. Together, they adjust the deadline to accommodate a more quality-driven approach.

4. **Use Time Management Techniques**: Emily employs the Pomodoro Technique, dedicating focused intervals to her work with short breaks in between. This helps maintain her concentration and reduces fatigue.
5. **Communicate Early and Often**: By keeping her team and supervisor in the loop about her progress and any potential hurdles, Emily ensures that expectations are managed and support is available when needed.
6. **Prepare for Interruptions**: Anticipating possible interruptions, Emily schedules buffer times throughout her days. This preparation helps her stay on track even when unexpected issues arise.
7. **Practice Self-care**: Despite the rush, Emily makes sure to step away for lunch breaks, stays hydrated, and does brief mindfulness exercises to clear her mind and reduce stress.

By adopting these strategies, tight deadlines become less intimidating. For Emily, and professionals everywhere, effective time management is key not only to meeting deadlines but also to maintaining a healthy balance that allows creativity and productivity to flourish without sacrificing personal well-being.

The Hidden Costs of Chronic Stress

While stress is an inevitable part of life, especially in the workplace, chronic stress can have profound, long-term effects on our health, productivity, and overall quality of life. But why do we often stay in this state longer than necessary? Sometimes, there are underlying 'payoffs' that keep us from seeking or implementing solutions. Understanding these can be crucial in turning our approach from merely coping to actively managing and reducing stress.

1. **Comfort in Familiarity**: Stress, especially in a high-pressure work environment, can become a familiar state. This familiarity sometimes feels safer than venturing into the unknown or trying new approaches to problem-solving. We might stick to known methods, even if they're inefficient, because they're predictable.
2. **Avoidance of Responsibility**: Being in a constant state of stress can, paradoxically, be used as an excuse for not taking on additional responsibilities or for underperformance. It can become a shield, protecting us from expectations to push boundaries or improve.
3. **Immediate Gratification**: Stress can lead to short-term coping behaviors that offer immediate relief but are detrimental in the long run, such as procrastination, overeating,

or neglecting health. These habits provide a temporary 'payoff' that makes us feel better in the moment, delaying more effective solution-finding.

4. **Sympathy and Attention**: Sometimes, being stressed garners sympathy from others, which can be comforting. This attention can serve as a form of validation or support, making the state of stress something that some might not be in a hurry to change.
5. **Identity and Self-Worth**: For some, being busy and stressed is tied to their sense of self-worth and identity. The idea of being 'the person who can handle it all' or 'the go-to person in a crisis' can be gratifying and can make one reluctant to seek help or adopt less stressful working habits.

The Payoff of Finding Solutions

Conversely, recognizing and addressing the root causes of stress can lead to significant payoffs:

- **Improved Health and Well-being**: Reducing stress improves physical health, reduces the risk of chronic diseases, and enhances emotional resilience.
- **Increased Productivity**: By managing stress effectively, you can improve concentration, decision-making, and creativity, leading to better work outcomes.

- **Enhanced Relationships**: Lower stress levels can lead to better interactions with colleagues, fostering a more supportive and collaborative work environment.
- **Greater Career Satisfaction**: Managing stress effectively can lead to greater job satisfaction and opportunities for advancement, as you're able to engage more fully with your work without the constant distraction of stress.

Knowing why we sometimes stick with stress can really motivate us to handle it better. By using good strategies to manage stress, we can improve how we feel and work every day. Instead of getting stuck in stress for small, short-term comforts, focusing on the big benefits of reducing stress can help us all enjoy our jobs more and do better at them. This way, we make our workplace a happier and more productive place for everyone.

Navigating the Complexities of Workplace Challenges

As we journey through our careers, we often encounter various hurdles that test our resilience and adaptability. Sometimes, the challenges aren't about the tasks themselves but about the environment in which we work. Lacking crucial information, feeling insecure about our job stability, or dealing with poor task delegation can make our daily responsibilities feel more daunting. Recognizing these stress triggers is the first step toward addressing them. Let's explore these common workplace issues and discover practical strategies to overcome them, ensuring that we not only survive but thrive in our professional environments.

Insufficient Information: The Stress of Not Knowing

Imagine being asked to paint a picture but not told what to paint or even given all the colors you need. This is how it feels to work without the necessary information. Not having the details you need to do your job can lead to a lot of stress. It's like walking through a maze blindfolded. You feel unsure about each step and worry about making mistakes.

Strategies to Enhance Communication and Information Flow:

1. **Regular Check-Ins:** Set up frequent meetings or check-ins with your team and managers to ensure everyone is on the same page and has the information they need.
2. **Clear Communication Channels:** Establish clear and open channels where team members can ask for information or help without hesitation.

3. **Knowledge Sharing Practices:** Encourage a culture where sharing knowledge is valued. Tools like shared digital workspaces can make it easy for everyone to access information when they need it.

Insecurity and Job Stability: The Undermining Fear

Feeling insecure in your job can be deeply unsettling. Whether it's due to changes in the company, market downturns, or rumors of layoffs, job insecurity can make you feel as if you're standing on shaky ground. This constant worry is more than just a professional concern—it can take a toll on your mental health, leading to anxiety or depression.

Building Confidence and Security in Your Role:

1. **Skill Development:** Continuously improve and update your skills. This not only makes you more valuable to your team but also boosts your confidence.
2. **Open Dialogue:** Have honest discussions with your supervisors about your role and future opportunities. This can help clarify expectations and reduce uncertainties.
3. **Focus on What You Control:** Concentrate on your performance and contributions. Excelling in your role can provide a sense of security and accomplishment.

Poor Task Delegation: The Chaos of Unclear Roles

When tasks are not clearly assigned, it can lead to confusion and overload, which are major sources of stress. Unclear roles can make you feel like you're doing everything but accomplishing nothing. This disorganization not only affects individual stress levels but can also impede the efficiency of the entire team.

Improving Task Delegation for Stress Reduction:

1. **Role Clarification Sessions:** Regular sessions to clarify roles and responsibilities can prevent misunderstandings and ensure everyone knows what is expected of them.
2. **Use of Delegation Tools:** Implementing task management tools can help track responsibilities and progress, ensuring tasks are evenly and clearly distributed.
3. **Feedback Loops:** Establish feedback mechanisms to continually improve the delegation process, allowing team members to express concerns and suggest improvements.

Simple Steps to Better Work Life

In our workplaces, knowing what to do, feeling secure in our jobs, and having clear tasks are very important. By talking regularly with our team, making sure everyone can easily ask for what they need, and clearly dividing the work, we can make our jobs less stressful and more enjoyable. These simple steps help us all do better together. As we keep improving how we share information, support each other, and organize our work, we not only make our days easier but also build a happier and more productive place for everyone.

Understanding the Deeper Effects of Stress

As we explore ways to manage stress, it's equally important to recognize how it affects us not just today but over time. Stress is more than just an immediate reaction to daily pressures; it has profound implications on our overall health and effectiveness at work.

Psychological Impact of Stress

Short-Term Effects: Initially, stress might manifest as mere irritations or fleeting moments of anxiety, much like the buzzing of a fly that distracts and frustrates. However, even these minor disturbances can impair our ability to focus, make decisions, and stay engaged in our tasks, subtly undermining our daily performance.

Long-Term Effects: If stress persists, it can evolve from a nuisance into a constant shadow, leading to more severe mental health conditions such as depression or anxiety. Like a river slowly carving a canyon, prolonged stress reshapes our mental landscape, often with lasting effects that can sap our joy and energy, leaving us feeling perpetually drained and disconnected.

Impact on Physical Health and Job Performance

Physical Health: The body keeps score when it comes to stress. Short-term, you might notice increased fatigue or muscle tension, signs that the body is in a state of high alert. Over the long haul, this continuous state of emergency can lead to critical health issues like heart disease or diabetes, profoundly affecting our longevity and quality of life.

Job Performance: Stress initially might spur us into action, pushing us to meet deadlines and tackle challenges. Yet, this burst of energy is fleeting. As stress becomes a regular visitor, our capacity to perform at our best wanes. Creativity dwindles, teamwork suffers, and our once sharp focus blurs, gradually eroding our professional life and the collective output of our teams.

Reflecting on Our Journey Towards Wellness

Recognizing the wide-reaching impacts of stress compels us to treat our stress management practices not just as optional, but as essential. Every step we take to mitigate stress is a step towards not only enhancing our personal health but also fostering a thriving, supportive work environment. By nurturing our well-being, we pave the way for sustained professional success and a more fulfilling life, both at work and beyond.

Coping Mechanisms and Tools for Managing Stress

Managing stress effectively involves a blend of immediate solutions and long-term strategies. By cultivating mindfulness, honing organizational skills, and seeking support when needed, we can not only navigate stressful situations more effectively but also build a foundation for sustained mental health and productivity.

Mindfulness and Relaxation Techniques

Mindfulness and relaxation techniques are powerful tools for calming the mind and body in moments of stress. These simple practices can help bring you back to a state of balance, easing tension and fostering a sense of peace.

- **Deep Breathing**: One of the quickest ways to reduce stress is through deep, controlled breathing. Try the 4-7-8 technique: inhale for four seconds, hold the breath for seven seconds, and exhale slowly for eight seconds. This helps reduce anxiety and brings your focus to the present moment.
- **Progressive Muscle Relaxation**: This involves tensing and then relaxing different muscle groups in your body. This technique not only helps relieve physical tension but also draws your attention away from the sources of stress.
- **Guided Imagery**: Visualize a peaceful scene, such as a beach or a quiet forest. Engage all your senses in this visualization to deepen the experience. This can provide a mental escape from stressful situations.

Organizational Skills

Enhancing your organizational skills can significantly reduce stress by making your workday more manageable and predictable.

- **Time Management**: Use tools like calendars and task lists to keep track of deadlines and appointments. Prioritizing tasks by urgency and importance can help you focus on what really needs to be done without feeling overwhelmed.

- **Declutter Your Workspace**: A tidy workspace can reduce mental clutter. Spend a few minutes at the end of each day organizing your desk, which can help you start the next day with a clearer mind.
- **Set Clear Goals**: Break larger tasks into smaller, manageable goals. This not only makes the task seem less daunting but also provides a clear roadmap to follow, reducing anxiety.

Seeking Support

No one has to manage stress alone. Seeking support from peers or professionals can provide relief and new strategies for handling pressure.

- **Talk to Colleagues**: Sharing your stressors with trusted colleagues can help you feel less isolated and may also lead to practical advice or solutions.
- **Professional Help**: If stress becomes overwhelming, consider seeking help from a mental health professional. They can offer strategies and tools tailored to your specific needs.
- **Support Groups**: Joining a support group where members share similar experiences

can provide a sense of community and mutual encouragement.

Empowering Ourselves Through Effective Stress Management

By integrating these coping mechanisms into our daily routines, we empower ourselves to handle stress with grace and resilience. Whether it's through mindfulness practices that bring us back to the present, organizational techniques that clear our path, or seeking support that reminds us we're not alone, each step is a move towards not just surviving but thriving in our personal and professional lives.

Cultivating Confidence Through the As-If Technique

In our daily lives, it's not uncommon to encounter situations that test our confidence and composure. Whether it's a challenging meeting, a public speaking engagement, or simply the need to uphold resilience in a tough moment, maintaining a sense of confidence is crucial. The As-If Technique is a powerful guided meditation that can help you harness and build this essential quality. By embodying confidence physically and mentally, you can transform your inner landscape to one of strength and self-assurance. Let's begin this exercise to not only visualize but also actualize a more confident you. Follow these steps to embrace and project the confidence you wish to feel.

As-If Technique for bringing back your energy:

Take a deep, slow breath in, filling your lungs completely, and then gently release it, letting go of any tension. Allow yourself to become fully present in this moment. Close your eyes if it feels right, and allow a gentle smile to play across your face. Sit or stand with your spine straight, shoulders pulled back slightly, and your chin tilted upwards just a touch – the posture of someone who is confident and in control.

Now, embody the posture of confidence. Hold yourself as if you are brimming with confidence as if every fibre of your being radiates self-assurance and poise. Feel your feet firmly planted on the ground, supporting you, grounding you in this state of power.

Shift your facial expression to match this state of confidence. Smooth your brow, relax your jaw, and let your eyes reflect a calm, assertive energy. Breathe in deeply, as if each breath draws in more confidence, filling you from within.

Begin to create an internal voice, a powerful, clear voice that asserts, 'My name is [Your Name], and I am filled with confidence.' Let this mantra echo within you, 'My name is [Your Name], and I am unstoppable.' Feel the truth of these words as you continue to breathe deeply, maintaining your confident posture and expression.

As you hold yourself in this state, notice the sensations of confidence permeating your being. Your spine supports you effortlessly, your shoulders are relaxed yet strong, and your facial muscles are relaxed, reflecting a serene yet powerful composure.

With every breath, let this feeling of confidence deepen. Imagine with each inhalation you're enhancing this state, and with each exhalation, you're releasing any remnants of doubt or insecurity.

Now, rub your hands together briskly, generating warmth and energy. Gently place them over your eyes, feeling the transfer of warmth and confidence into your very vision, as if you are seeing the world through the lens of your newfound confidence.

When you feel ready, gradually lower your hands and open your eyes, carrying this sense of confidence with you. Remind yourself, 'I am [Your Name], and I am confident.' Carry this confidence into your day, knowing you can return to this state anytime you wish.

Carrying Confidence and Calm into Every Aspect of Life

With a deeper understanding of how to manage stress through mindfulness, structured planning, and supportive networks, we are better equipped to navigate the complexities of our professional lives. These tools not only help us handle stress in the moment but also empower us to build resilience over time. As we enhance our ability to stay calm and organized under pressure, we might notice changes not just at work but also at home.

Our next exploration takes us into the seamless flow between our work and personal lives. The Ripple Effect examines how the stresses and triumphs of our professional experiences do not end at the office door—they accompany us home, influencing our interactions with family and friends, and vice versa. In the upcoming chapter, "The Ripple Effect: From Work to Home and Back Again," we will uncover the profound ways our personal and professional lives intertwine, impacting each other. By understanding this dynamic, we aim to foster a more harmonious balance that enhances our well-being across all environments.

Chapter 3

The Ripple Effect: From Work to Home and Back Again

Understanding the Interconnectivity of Work and Home Life

The boundary between our work and personal lives is often more porous than we might like to admit. Stress, whether originating at work or home, does not neatly confine itself to one area of our lives but tends to spill over, creating ripples that affect everything it touches. Recognizing this interconnectivity is crucial for managing stress effectively and maintaining harmony in both professional and personal spheres.

The Impact of Work Stress on Family Life

Work stress can come home with us at the end of the day, influencing our moods, behaviors, and interactions with family members. When preoccupied with a difficult project or unresolved workplace issues, we may find ourselves less patient, more irritable, or simply too drained to engage fully with our loved ones. This can lead to misunderstandings, conflicts, and a general sense of dissatisfaction within the family environment.

Children are particularly sensitive to changes in a parent's mood and behavior. A parent under stress may be less responsive or more punitive, which can affect a child's emotional and behavioral development. Partners can also feel neglected or undervalued when work stress monopolizes time and energy that might otherwise be dedicated to relationship nurturing and joint activities.

How Personal Life Stress Affects the Workplace

Conversely, stress that originates at home does not simply dissipate once we step into the workplace. Personal challenges such as marital difficulties, health issues, or parenting struggles can occupy our thoughts, reducing our focus and productivity at work. This distraction can lead to mistakes, missed deadlines, and reduced quality of work, which may compound stress by creating additional pressures and job insecurity.

Moreover, stress from personal life can lead to increased absenteeism or presenteeism (being physically present at work but mentally distracted). It can also make us less cooperative and more conflict-prone with colleagues, further deteriorating our work environment.

Understanding the Psychological Drivers Behind the Ripple Effect

While it may seem counterintuitive to carry stress from one domain of our lives to another, there are underlying psychological mechanisms that often propel this behavior. Exploring these can help us understand why we might continue to perpetuate this cycle, despite its negative effects.

1. **Psychological Consistency and Homeostasis:** Humans naturally seek consistency in their emotional states and behaviors across different contexts. This drive for psychological homeostasis means that if we are stressed in one area of our life, we may subconsciously maintain this stress level across other areas to reduce internal conflict and maintain a sense of uniformity. This can explain why stress in the workplace can seep into home life and vice versa.
2. **Identity and Self-Concept:** Our identities are often closely tied to our roles both at work and at home. When these roles are threatened by external stressors, we may carry stress across these boundaries in an attempt to protect and reinforce our self-concept. For example, a person who identifies strongly as a provider may carry financial stress from work home, affecting family interactions.

3. **Lack of Compartmentalization Skills:** Not everyone has the ability to compartmentalize their lives effectively. This psychological skill helps individuals to keep different facets of their lives separate from each other. Without strong compartmentalization skills, it's easier for emotions and stress to flow freely across the boundaries of work and home.
4. **Cognitive Load and Overwhelm:** When individuals face high levels of stress, their cognitive load increases, which can overwhelm their mental resources. This overwhelm makes it harder to manage thoughts and emotions effectively, leading to a spill-over of stress. This often results in a diminished capacity to engage in cognitive switching necessary to leave work stress at work and home stress at home.
5. **Negative Reinforcement:** Continuing the cycle of stress can also be inadvertently reinforced. For instance, if bringing work stress home leads to sympathy and additional support from family, it might reinforce the behavior subconsciously. Similarly, showing signs of personal stress at work might lead to lower expectations from colleagues, which can temporarily ease work demands.

Understanding the deep-seated psychological reasons behind why we carry stress across the different areas of our lives gives us valuable insights into how to manage it better. By applying targeted strategies to enhance our psychological flexibility and strengthen our boundaries, we can minimize the ripple effects of stress. This not only leads to a more balanced life but also enriches our interactions both at home and at work, ultimately contributing to our overall well-being and success.

The Payoffs of Addressing the Ripple Effect

Addressing the ripple effect of stress not only improves our well-being but also enhances our relationships at home and our performance at work. When we manage to keep stress from overwhelming one area of our lives, we are more present and effective in all others. This balance can lead to:

- **Increased Job Satisfaction**: By not allowing personal stress to spill over into the workplace, we can focus better, achieve more, and feel more satisfied with our job.
- **Healthier Family Dynamics**: Similarly, by leaving work stress at the office, we can be more attentive, supportive, and engaged with our family, fostering a healthier home environment.

Coping Mechanisms and Tools for Managing the Ripple Effect

Recognizing psychological factors is the first step toward breaking the cycle. Here are some targeted strategies to help manage and compartmentalize stress more effectively:

1. **Mindfulness and Awareness Practices:** Becoming more aware of our stress triggers and our responses to them can help us start to control these reactions. Practices like mindfulness meditation can increase this awareness and help us remain centered.
2. **Developing Stronger Boundaries:** Actively working on setting and maintaining clear boundaries between work and home can help prevent the flow of stress between them. This might include physical boundaries, like a dedicated workspace, or temporal boundaries, like defined work hours.
3. **Enhancing Emotional Regulation Skills:** Techniques such as deep breathing, progressive muscle relaxation, or even short walks can help manage emotional responses and reduce the immediate impact of stress.
4. **Compartmentalization**: Learning to compartmentalize can be a valuable skill, helping to keep work stress from invading home life and vice versa. This involves

setting clear boundaries between work and personal life, such as not checking work emails during family meals or setting aside specific times to discuss work issues at home.

5. **Communication Skills**: Open and honest communication with family members and colleagues about the stresses we're experiencing can help mitigate misunderstandings and garner support. Discussing work stress with family can help them understand your challenges and offer support, while discussing personal stress with a supervisor can lead to accommodations that might reduce work pressure.
6. **Regular Physical Activity**: Engaging in regular physical activity is a proven stress reliever and can help maintain a clear separation between our professional and personal lives. Exercise not only improves physical health but also boosts mental clarity and mood, making it easier to handle stress.
7. **Seeking Professional Help:** Sometimes, working with a psychologist or therapist can provide the tools and insights needed to develop better compartmentalization skills and manage stress more effectively.

Embracing Harmony: Navigating the Ripple Effect

As we reflect on the insights gained from exploring the ripple effect of stress between our work and home lives, we recognize the profound impact our environments have on each other. Addressing this interconnected stress is not just about improving isolated moments but about enhancing our overall quality of life. By actively managing how stress travels between our professional and personal spheres, we create more supportive environments for ourselves and those around us.

The strategies and understanding developed in this chapter not only help us mitigate stress but also enrich our relationships and boost our professional efficacy. Mindfulness, clear communication, and well-defined boundaries do more than just limit stress—they foster resilience, allowing us to thrive in all aspects of life. As we learn to balance and compartmentalize our experiences of stress, we set the stage for sustained personal growth and deeper fulfillment.

Looking Ahead: Understanding the Comprehensive Impact of Stress

Having explored the ripple effect of stress, it's crucial to broaden our perspective even further. Our next chapter, "The Cost of Stress: Physical, Emotional, and Organizational Toll," delves into the broader implications of stress. We will examine how persistent stress not only affects our physical and emotional health but also impacts the overall health of the organizations we are part of. By understanding these wider effects, we can better advocate for changes that promote well-being across all areas of our lives, from our physical health to our professional environments. Join us as we continue to uncover the full scope of stress's impact and learn more about how we can collectively work towards a healthier, more balanced future.

Chapter 4

The Cost of Stress: Physical, Emotional, and Organizational Toll

"Stress is like spice – in the right proportion, it enhances the flavor of a dish. Too little produces a bland, dull meal; too much may choke you." - Donald Tubesing

This insightful analogy by Donald Tubesing highlights the dual nature of stress. While a certain amount can be stimulating and motivating, too much stress can become harmful, impacting not just our personal health but also our professional environments. In this chapter, we will delve into the broader implications of stress, examining its effects on our physical health, emotional well-being, and the overall health of the organizations we are part of. Understanding these impacts is critical, as it emphasizes the need for effective management strategies to mitigate stress's adverse effects and enhance our overall quality of life. Through exploring these areas, we aim to provide insights and tools that support a healthier, more balanced approach to both personal and organizational development.

Donald Tubesing was an author and speaker focused on stress management and wellness. He co-founded Whole Person Associates, a company dedicated to helping individuals achieve better health and balance. Tubesing authored several books on managing stress and improving well-being.

Personal Reflection: Navigating Through Stress Toward Resilience

In 2013, I found myself at a crucial juncture in both my professional life and my role as a parent. With a rising career and recognition within my professional circle, my ambitions were expanding. During this period, my second child, Abdullah, began to walk. Unlike my first child, Faizan, who was primarily nurtured by my father during his early years, I was deeply involved in Abdullah's early stages. This new emotional experience introduced a novel set of stresses related to parenting.

As I observed Abdullah's first steps, the reality of my responsibilities as a father intensified my fears about providing for my growing family. The job that once seemed adequate now appeared insufficient for their future needs. This worry triggered a cascade of stress that began to overshadow my life. It led me to make several poor financial decisions, adding further strain and enhancing my stress levels. My physical health, once a point of personal pride, began to suffer. Despite being a fit, dynamic 40-year-old, I developed high blood pressure, an ailment I never anticipated facing at this stage of life.

The stress did not only affect me physically; it also impacted my professional demeanor. Known for my calm, my growing irritability began to close doors, leading to missed opportunities. My temper, sharpened by stress, contributed to a significant career setback—I lost my job and faced two months of unemployment. This period, however, became a critical time for introspection and self-assessment. It was during these months that I truly understood the severe implications of unmanaged stress and began to seek methods to handle it more effectively.

This personal crisis, coupled with the challenges brought on by the COVID-19 pandemic years later, tested my stress management strategies. However, having learned from my earlier experiences, I approached these challenges with a different mindset. My previous journey through job loss and health issues had equipped me with the resilience and tools necessary to navigate through adversity. By applying mindfulness, seeking professional guidance, and maintaining physical health, I managed not only to survive the stress but to thrive despite it.

Connecting Personal Experience to Broader Implications

My story underscores the critical nature of recognizing and addressing the physical costs of stress. It demonstrates how unchecked stress can lead to severe health issues, affect emotional well-being, and drastically alter one's career trajectory. It also highlights the importance of proactive stress management, which can transform potential crises into opportunities for growth and development.

As we continue to explore the toll stress can take on our lives, both personal stories and scientific research guide us toward effective strategies for managing stress. By understanding the deep connection between our physical health and stress, we can better prepare ourselves to handle the challenges life throws our way, ensuring we not only maintain our health but also enhance our overall life satisfaction.

Physical Costs of Stress

Stress is not just a mental challenge; it manifests physically, influencing our entire body's functioning and potentially leading to serious health conditions.

Understanding the Body's Stress Response

The body's natural reaction to perceived threats or demands is the fight-or-flight response, activated by the release of hormones like adrenaline and cortisol.

These hormones prepare the body to either confront or flee from the threat. Physically, this response increases heart rate, elevates blood pressure, and boosts energy supplies. While essential for survival in acute situations, when this response is triggered too frequently or for prolonged periods, it becomes harmful, disrupting normal bodily functions and increasing the risk of health issues.

Long-Term Health Consequences

Chronic activation of the stress response can lead to several serious health problems:

- **Cardiovascular Disease:** Continuous high levels of stress hormones can lead to increased blood pressure and heart rate, raising the risk of hypertension and heart disease.
- **Diabetes:** Stress can influence blood sugar levels, contributing to the development or worsening of diabetes by making it harder to control blood sugar effectively.
- **Weakened Immune System:** Prolonged stress suppresses immune responses, making the body more vulnerable to infections and slowing down recovery times from illness or injury.

Immediate Physical Symptoms

The immediate physical symptoms of stress serve as early warning signs that our body is under duress:

- **Headaches:** Stress can trigger tension headaches or migraines due to muscle tension or changes in chemical balances in the brain.
- **Muscle Tension and Pain:** Stress often leads to involuntary muscle tension, particularly in the neck, shoulders, and back, resulting in pain and discomfort.
- **Fatigue:** Despite potentially causing an initial surge in energy, chronic stress can lead to depletion of energy reserves, resulting in persistent fatigue.

By understanding how stress affects the body both in the short term and long term, we can take proactive steps to manage it effectively and mitigate its impact on our health. Recognizing these signs and symptoms as they occur is crucial in taking timely action to reduce stress and improve overall well-being.

Emotional Costs of Stress

While the physical impacts of stress are highly visible, the emotional costs can be equally profound but sometimes less recognized. These emotional effects not only deteriorate one's quality of life but can also lead to significant mental health challenges.

Mental Health Impact

Chronic stress acts as a potent catalyst for various mental health issues:

- **Anxiety:** Persistent stress keeps the body in a heightened state of alertness, contributing to an ongoing sense of fear and worry that characterizes anxiety disorders.
- **Depression:** Long-term stress may lead to depression by overwhelming the individual and creating feelings of helplessness and hopelessness.
- **Burnout:** Particularly relevant in occupational settings, burnout is a state of emotional, physical, and mental exhaustion caused by excessive and prolonged stress. It results in decreased motivation and efficacy within the workplace.

Exploring these impacts allows us to understand how integral stress management is to maintaining mental health and why interventions should be a priority in both personal and professional contexts.

Quality of Life

The pervasive nature of stress significantly affects one's overall life satisfaction and emotional well-being:

- Persistent stress can erode the joy and satisfaction derived from daily activities and relationships, leading to diminished personal happiness and fulfillment.
- It can also impair one's ability to maintain positive social interactions and engage in meaningful personal projects, further reducing life quality.

Coping Mechanisms

Individuals adopt various strategies to cope with stress, which can have long-term effects on their health and well-being:

Healthy Coping Mechanisms:

- **Exercise:** Regular physical activity is one of the most effective ways to reduce stress. It helps release endorphins, improves mood, and can act as a temporary distraction from daily worries.
- **Mindfulness and Meditation:** These practices help center the mind and reduce anxiety by focusing on the present moment and cultivating a sense of peace.
- **Seeking Social Support:** Talking things out with friends, family, or a professional can provide emotional relief and offer new perspectives on stressful situations.

Unhealthy Coping Mechanisms:

- **Substance Use:** Turning to drugs, alcohol, or excessive caffeine as a way to manage stress can lead to addiction and compound the existing stress with additional health problems.
- **Overeating or Under-eating:** Stress can lead to changes in appetite and eating behaviors, which may result in significant weight gain or loss and associated health issues.

- **Avoidance and Withdrawal:** Avoiding stressful situations may provide temporary relief, but it often increases stress in the long term as the underlying issues remain unresolved.

Understanding both healthy and unhealthy coping mechanisms not only helps individuals make informed choices about how to manage stress but also highlights the importance of fostering healthy habits as part of regular stress management practices.

Strategies for Mitigation

Successfully mitigating the effects of stress involves adopting strategies that can be implemented on an individual level. Each person's approach to stress management may vary, but incorporating a mix of time management, mindfulness, and physical exercise can provide a robust foundation for reducing stress and enhancing overall well-being.

Individual Strategies

1. **Time Management:**

   - **Prioritize Tasks:** Start by identifying what needs to be done and categorize tasks by importance and urgency. This helps in focusing on what truly matters, reducing the overwhelm from a cluttered to-do list.

- **Break Tasks into Smaller Steps:** Large projects can seem daunting and stress-inducing. Breaking them into manageable parts can make them feel less intimidating and more achievable.
- **Use Tools and Technology:** Leveraging tools like digital calendars, task management apps, or even simple to-do lists can help keep track of responsibilities and deadlines, alleviating the stress that comes from trying to remember everything.

2. **Mindfulness and Meditation:**

- **Daily Practice:** Integrating mindfulness into daily routines can help center thoughts and reduce the anxiety that comes from constant stress. Even short periods of meditation can improve mental clarity and emotional stability.
- **Breathing Exercises:** Simple breathing techniques, such as diaphragmatic breathing or the 4-7-8 method, can be particularly effective in moments of acute stress, helping to calm the mind and reduce physical symptoms of stress.
- **Mindful Walking:** Incorporating mindfulness into regular activities like walking can transform routine actions into

meditative practices, promoting relaxation and a calm mind.

3. **Physical Exercise:**

    - **Regular Activity:** Engaging in regular physical activity is one of the most effective ways to combat stress. Exercise not only improves physical health but also helps release endorphins, chemicals in the brain that act as natural painkillers and mood elevators.
    - **Yoga:** Yoga combines physical poses with controlled breathing and meditation, making it an excellent choice for stress relief. Its focus on balance and flexibility can also help reduce physical tension associated with stress.
    - **Outdoor Activities:** Activities like hiking, cycling, or even gardening can increase one's connection with nature, which has been shown to lower stress levels and improve mood.

Implementing these strategies can significantly enhance your ability to manage stress effectively, leading to better health, increased productivity, and greater overall happiness. By taking proactive steps toward stress management, you're not only mitigating the immediate impacts of stress but also building resilience against future challenges. Whether it's refining your time management skills, incorporating mindfulness into your daily routine, or engaging in regular physical activities, each step you take is an investment in your long-term well-being. Start today, and transform how you handle stress, opening up a path to a more balanced and fulfilling life.

Case Studies and Real-World Examples

Let's dive into the real world where clever stress management isn't just theory—it's action! Below, you'll find two riveting case studies that showcase exactly how people like you and organizations just like yours have successfully tackled stress head-on. Get ready to discover actionable strategies that you can apply today to manage stress more effectively. Let's explore these success stories together:

Case Study 1: Personal Stress Management in the Tech Industry

Background: Jane, a software developer at a leading tech company, found herself overwhelmed by the fast-paced and demanding nature of her job. Despite loving her work, the long hours and high stakes began to take a toll on her mental health.

Challenge: Jane started experiencing severe anxiety, which affected her productivity and personal life. She knew she needed to find a way to manage her stress before it escalated further.

Solution: Jane decided to prioritize her well-being by:

- **Setting Boundaries:** She began strictly delineating her work hours and made it a point to unplug from all work-related communications after 6 PM.
- **Mindfulness Meditation:** She attended a mindfulness workshop offered by her employer and started practicing meditation for 15 minutes every morning.
- **Regular Exercise:** Jane joined a local gym and committed to attending fitness classes three times a week.

Outcome: After three months, Jane noticed a significant reduction in her anxiety levels. Her productivity at work returned to its previous high standard, and her personal relationships improved. Her case demonstrates how individual actions can dramatically influence personal stress management.

Case Study 2: Organizational Stress Management in Healthcare

Background: A regional hospital was experiencing high turnover rates among its nursing staff, largely due to job-related stress and burnout.

Challenge: The hospital needed to address the systemic issues causing stress to retain skilled nurses and ensure high-quality patient care.

Solution: The hospital administration implemented several key initiatives:

- **Wellness Programs:** Introduced a wellness program that included stress management workshops and free yoga classes for staff.
- **Scheduling Changes:** Revamped the shift scheduling system to allow for more flexible work hours and longer breaks between shifts.
- **Support Systems:** Established a peer support system where nurses could discuss their challenges in a supportive environment.

Outcome: These initiatives led to a noticeable decrease in staff turnover and burnout rates. Employee satisfaction scores improved, and there was a marked enhancement in patient care outcomes. This case study highlights how organizational strategies can effectively mitigate workplace stress.

Reference for Further Reading:

- *Harvard Business Review* article, "How Companies Can Reduce the Stress of Working in High-Stakes Industries" provides additional insights into strategies implemented in high-pressure work environments.
- *Journal of Clinical Nursing* study, "Impact of Workplace Wellness Programs on Nursing Staff," which details similar interventions and their results in healthcare settings.

These case studies serve as powerful examples of how both personal initiatives and organizational strategies can effectively manage and reduce stress, leading to improved well-being and productivity. By examining these cases, individuals and organizations can gain practical ideas for implementing similar stress management practices in their own contexts.

Introspect yourself:

As you reflect on the insights from Chapter 4, "The Cost of Stress: Physical, Emotional, and Organizational Toll," these questions are designed to deepen your understanding and help you apply the knowledge to your own life. Take a moment to consider how stress manifests for you personally, evaluate your coping strategies, and think about the changes you can make to enhance your resilience.

Engaging with these questions will allow you to connect the concepts discussed to real-life situations, empowering you to manage stress more effectively.

1. **Self-Reflection on Stress Response**: Think about a recent stressful situation. Did you notice any physical or emotional signs that were discussed in this chapter, such as increased heart rate, anxiety, or irritability? How did you respond to these signs?
2. **Assessing Coping Strategies**: Reflect on the coping mechanisms you currently use to manage stress. Which ones do you find most effective, and are there any that might be causing more harm than good? How might you replace less healthy strategies with more beneficial ones?
3. **Impact of Stress on Daily Life**: In what ways has stress affected your personal relationships or job performance in the past? Considering what you've learned, what steps can you take to minimize its impact moving forward?
4. **Connection Between Physical and Emotional Health**: How has your understanding of the link between physical symptoms and emotional stress changed after reading this chapter? Can you think of a time when physical symptoms alerted you to emotional stress?

5. **Long-Term Changes**: What long-term changes are you considering implementing in your life after learning about the physical and emotional costs of stress? How can these changes improve both your personal and professional life?

As we wrap up this chapter, we've uncovered just how deeply stress can seep into every corner of our lives, impacting our health, our happiness, and our work. Armed with the strategies we've explored, you're now better equipped to turn the tide against stress, enhancing not only your well-being but also your effectiveness in every role you play.

Looking ahead, our next chapter, "Empowerment Through Self-Esteem: Confronting and Overcoming Insecurities," promises to take us deeper into the transformative power of self-esteem. We'll discover how building our inner strength can not only buffer us against stress but also empower us to rise above the dynamics of power and control that challenge us. Ready to unlock a more confident and controlled version of yourself? Let's continue our journey, transforming challenges into opportunities for growth and empowerment. Join me as we step into a world where self-esteem becomes our greatest ally against the trials of life.

Chapter 5:

Empowerment Through Self-Esteem: Confronting and Overcoming Insecurities

Self-esteem is not just about feeling good about oneself; it's a fundamental aspect of our mental health and emotional resilience. High self-esteem acts as a buffer against the stresses of life, while low self-esteem can make us more vulnerable to the negative dynamics of power and control, both personally and professionally. This chapter delves into how low self-esteem contributes to stress and outlines practical strategies to enhance self-esteem, empowering us to navigate our world with confidence and control.

Understanding the Paradox: Why We Sometimes Choose Low Self-Esteem

It might seem counterintuitive, but there are psychological reasons why our brains might cling to low self-esteem, despite its negative consequences. This adherence often stems from perceived short-term benefits that serve to protect us from potential emotional harm.

1. **Familiarity and Comfort Zone:** Low self-esteem can be a familiar state to many, and there is comfort in the familiar, even when it's painful. Staying in this zone avoids the uncertainty and risk that come with stepping into new, potentially rewarding experiences where failure is a possibility.
2. **Avoidance of Responsibility:** Maintaining low self-esteem can serve as a shield from taking on greater responsibilities or challenges. If you don't believe in your capability, you might avoid situations where you're expected to step up, thereby reducing the fear of failure.
3. **Protection From Disappointment:** When you don't expect much from yourself, you protect yourself from the disappointment of not meeting higher expectations. This defense mechanism keeps you in a lower-risk, lower-reward scenario, but it also prevents the feelings of letdown that come from not achieving ambitious goals.
4. **Sympathy and Support:** Sometimes, individuals with low self-esteem receive more emotional support from others because their vulnerabilities are apparent. This external validation can reinforce low self-esteem as it provides comfort and attention,

making the effort to build self-esteem seem less appealing.

5. **Control Over Failures:** If someone with low self-esteem fails, it can ironically confirm their own views about their limitations. This self-fulfilling prophecy allows them to feel a sense of control over the outcome, even if it's negative. "I knew I couldn't do it" can be a strangely reassuring conclusion, reinforcing their existing worldview.

Understanding these underlying reasons can be the first step in recognizing how low self-esteem might be serving you in a limited, though detrimental, way. This awareness is crucial as it paves the way for addressing and gradually dismantling these psychological barriers, allowing for the development of a healthier self-esteem.

The Impact of Low Self-Esteem on Stress

Low self-esteem often sets the stage for stress by influencing how we perceive and react to challenges:

- **Increased Vulnerability to Stress:** Individuals with low self-esteem may doubt their abilities and value, which heightens anxiety and susceptibility to stress in challenging situations.

- **Poor Coping Strategies:** Those with low self-esteem are more likely to resort to ineffective or harmful stress management techniques, such as avoidance, denial, or substance abuse.
- **Sensitivity to Criticism:** A lack of confidence can lead to an increased sensitivity to criticism, real or perceived, which can trigger stress and impede performance and relationships.

Enhancing Self-Esteem: Strategies for Empowerment

Building self-esteem is a dynamic process that involves recognizing your intrinsic worth, overcoming negative self-perceptions, and developing a healthier, more empowered self-image. Here are effective strategies to boost your self-esteem:

1. **Self-Awareness and Positive Self-Talk:**

   - Cultivate self-awareness by reflecting on your thoughts, emotions, and reactions. Identify patterns of negative self-talk and challenge these thoughts with evidence of your competencies and achievements.
   - Engage in positive self-affirmations daily to reinforce your strengths and value. This practice can gradually replace negative

thoughts with a more positive outlook on your abilities.

2. **Achievement and Skill Development:**

    - Set achievable goals that align with your interests and values. Accomplishing these goals will provide tangible proof of your capabilities, enhancing your sense of self-efficacy.
    - Continuously develop new skills and hobbies. Skill mastery not only improves self-esteem but also provides a constructive outlet for managing stress.

3. **Social Connections and Support:**

    - Invest in relationships that make you feel valued and appreciated. Positive interactions with friends, family, and colleagues can reinforce your self-worth.
    - Seek out groups or communities where you can share experiences and support each other in self-esteem building activities.

4. **Professional Help:**

    - Consider therapy or counseling if low self-esteem is significantly impacting your life. Cognitive Behavioral Therapy (CBT) and other therapeutic approaches can be very effective in addressing deep-seated negative beliefs about oneself.

The Payoff: A Life Empowered by Self-Esteem

Enhancing your self-esteem transforms not just how you handle stress, but how you approach life itself. With higher self-esteem, you are better equipped to assert your needs, make healthier choices, and pursue opportunities without the handicap of self-doubt. This empowerment leads to:

- **Reduced Stress:** As your self-esteem increases, your overall stress levels can decrease, resulting in fewer physical and emotional health issues.
- **Improved Relationships:** High self-esteem enables more authentic and positive interactions with others, enriching both personal and professional relationships.
- **Greater Professional Success:** Confidence in your abilities allows you to take on challenges and seize opportunities that can lead to career advancement.

As we conclude this exploration of self-esteem and its profound impact on our lives, it becomes clear that nurturing our self-esteem is not merely an act of personal development but a crucial strategy for stress management. By understanding and addressing the root causes of low self-esteem, we equip ourselves with the tools to face life's challenges with a stronger sense of self-worth and resilience.

We've delved into the reasons why some may unconsciously cling to low self-esteem and how such a stance can adversely impact our ability to manage stress effectively. We also explored practical steps to build and maintain healthy self-esteem, from engaging in positive self-talk and setting achievable goals to fostering supportive social connections and seeking professional help when necessary.

The empowerment gained through enhanced self-esteem extends far beyond mere stress reduction. It catalyzes a transformative process where you not only meet life's demands more effectively but also engage with the world in a more assertive and positive manner. High self-esteem enables you to navigate through life's ups and downs with grace and fortitude, leading to improved relationships, better job performance, and a more fulfilling life.

As we move forward, let us shift our focus to a broader perspective in the next chapter, "Holistic Wellness: Integrating Lifestyle Changes for Stress Reduction." Here, we will explore how integrating physical activity, balanced nutrition, and mental health practices into your daily routine can create a comprehensive wellness strategy. This holistic approach not only supports the gains made in building self-esteem but also fortifies your overall ability to manage stress in a dynamic and ever-changing world. Join me as we discover how to weave these elements together to form a resilient tapestry of well-being that supports and enhances every aspect of your life.

Chapter 6

Holistic Wellness: Integrating Lifestyle Changes for Stress Reduction

"Take care of your body. It's the only place you have to live." — Jim Rohn

Embracing the wisdom of Jim Rohn, this chapter, "Holistic Wellness: Integrating Lifestyle Changes for Stress Reduction," invites you on a transformative journey to revolutionize your approach to health and stress management. Here, we explore how integrating physical activity, balanced nutrition, and mental health practices into your daily life isn't just about maintaining wellness but about enhancing your entire existence.

Imagine a life where stress is not a roadblock but a manageable aspect of your day, countered by healthful practices that nurture your body, mind, and spirit. This isn't about sporadic health kicks or temporary diets; it's about building a consistent, enjoyable lifestyle that empowers you to thrive under pressure and face challenges with resilience.

In the following pages, we will dive into the powerful synergy of holistic wellness, combining cutting-edge research with practical strategies that you can implement right now. Whether you're aiming to overhaul your diet, establish a regular exercise routine, or deepen your mental health practices, this chapter will equip you with the tools to create a balanced, fulfilling life.

Ready to transform your approach to stress and elevate your overall vitality? Let's embark on this journey together, discovering how comprehensive lifestyle changes can lead to profound improvements in your stress levels and overall life satisfaction.

Personal Reflection: Transforming Perspective and Embracing Holistic Wellness

Before embracing holistic wellness, my professional life as an inspector deeply influenced my personal interactions. In my career, I was trained to scrutinize and identify faults, a skill necessary for ensuring quality and safety in work environments. However, this mindset spilled over into my personal life in ways I hadn't anticipated. I found myself constantly critiquing others, often negatively, striving to prove my ideas superior and dismissing those of people around me. This critical approach led me to conflict and strained many of my personal relationships, even to the point where I began losing connections with friends and family members.

Despite the professional success this critical eye afforded me, my personal life suffered. I was proud of my ability to spot flaws, yet deep inside, I sensed something was amiss. Was it possible that I was the only one right, and everyone else was wrong? This question lingered in my mind until I encountered two pivotal mentors: Sheikh Mohammed Al-Naqvi and Dr. YS Rathore. Their wisdom and guidance sparked a significant transformation in my approach to life.

From Sheikh Mohammed Al-Naqvi, I learned the power of introspection and the importance of questioning my own beliefs and behaviors rather than just those of others. Dr. YS Rathore introduced me to the concept of holistic wellness, which emphasizes not only physical health but also mental and emotional well-being. They taught me that effective criticism isn't just about finding faults but about fostering growth and improvement, both in oneself and others.

This shift in perspective was revolutionary. I began to see others not as adversaries but as allies, as members of a larger community to which I also belonged. By applying the principles of holistic wellness, I learned to balance my critical nature with empathy and constructive feedback, transforming how I interacted with the world around me.

The result was profound. Not only did I become more successful professionally—known for my fair and effective inspection skills—I also rebuilt old bridges and formed new relationships. People now see me not just as a skilled inspector but as a supportive colleague and friend. The stress that once overwhelmed me due to constant conflict has significantly diminished. Now, I manage stress with ease, using it as an opportunity to foster better understanding and cooperation.

In integrating holistic wellness into my life, I have found that stress does not have to be a barrier but can be a gateway to personal growth and improved relationships. This journey of transformation shows that when we broaden our perspectives and adopt a holistic approach to life, we not only enhance our own well-being but also enrich the lives of those around us. As we continue to explore holistic wellness in this chapter, let us consider how each aspect of our lives contributes to our overall health and how we, too, can turn our challenges into opportunities for growth and connection.

Key Components of Holistic Wellness

Holistic wellness encompasses more than just one aspect of health; it integrates physical, nutritional, and mental components to form a comprehensive approach to stress reduction and overall well-being. Each component plays a critical role in enhancing our ability to manage stress effectively and live a balanced, healthy life.

Physical Health: The Role of Regular Physical Activity

Regular physical activity is a cornerstone of holistic wellness and plays a pivotal role in managing stress. Engaging in regular exercise helps to release endorphins, often known as the body's natural painkillers and mood elevators. These biochemical changes in the brain contribute to improved moods and a general sense of well-being.

Beyond biochemical impacts, physical activity also helps to:

- **Reduce stress hormones** such as adrenaline and cortisol, which lowers overall stress levels and anxiety.
- **Improve sleep quality**, which is often negatively affected by stress. Better sleep helps regulate mood, improve brain function, and enhance overall health.
- **Increase resilience** by strengthening the body's ability to respond to and recover from stress. Regular exercise builds physical strength and endurance, which can make daily stressors more manageable.

Nutrition: The Impact of a Balanced Diet

Nutrition plays a critical role not only in physical health but also in mental and emotional well-being. A balanced diet provides the necessary nutrients that the brain and body need to function optimally, which is crucial for managing stress. Key aspects of a stress-reducing diet include:

- **Complex carbohydrates** like whole grains, fruits, and vegetables, which can boost serotonin levels in the brain and stabilize blood sugar levels.
- **Lean proteins** such as fish, poultry, and legumes, which can increase dopamine and norepinephrine levels, enhancing mood and alertness.
- **Healthy fats**, especially omega-3 fatty acids found in fish and flaxseeds, which are known to reduce the symptoms of stress and anxiety.
- **Adequate hydration**, which helps in the production of cortisol and can reduce stress.

Maintaining a balanced diet not only supports physical health but also impacts mental clarity and emotional stability, making it easier to handle stress.

Mental Health: Mindfulness, Meditation, and Sleep

Mental health practices such as mindfulness, meditation, and ensuring adequate sleep are vital components of holistic wellness. These practices help to cultivate a state of mental and emotional balance by:

- **Reducing rumination and worry**, which are often heightened by stress. Mindfulness and meditation encourage a focus on the present moment, reducing overthinking and anxiety.
- **Enhancing emotional resilience** by providing tools to manage and reduce stress actively. Regular meditation has been shown to decrease the density of brain tissue associated with anxiety and stress.
- **Improving sleep quality** by promoting relaxation and helping to break the cycle of stress-related insomnia. Adequate sleep is essential for cognitive function, mood regulation, and physical health—all critical for stress management.

Incorporating these mental health practices into daily life can significantly reduce the impact of stress, fostering a sense of calm and control even in challenging situations. When we weave together physical activity, nutrition, and mental health practices into our daily lives, holistic wellness transcends from being just an idea to becoming a practical blueprint for a healthier and more balanced existence. As we progress through this chapter, we'll delve deeper into how each of these elements not only helps us manage stress more effectively but also enriches our overall well-being. This integrated approach lays a solid foundation for enduring positive change, enabling us to navigate life's challenges with greater ease and resilience.

Physical Activity and Stress Reduction

Types of Activities: Physical exercise is a key component in managing stress, suitable for various fitness levels. Here are some recommended activities:

- **For Beginners:** Walking, light yoga, and stretching are excellent starting points for building fitness.
- **Intermediate Level:** Jogging, cycling, moderate yoga, and swimming provide a good middle ground for those with some fitness experience.
- **Advanced Level:** High-intensity interval training (HIIT), advanced yoga, and competitive sports are suitable for individuals seeking more challenging workouts.

Benefits: Physical activities help in reducing stress physiologically by:

- **Releasing Endorphins:** These are the body's natural painkillers and mood elevators.
- **Reducing Stress Hormones:** Exercise reduces levels of the body's stress hormones, such as adrenaline and cortisol.
- **Improving Sleep:** Regular physical activity can help you sleep better, which can reduce stress.

4. Nutritional Wellness

Essential Nutrients: Certain nutrients play crucial roles in managing stress:

- **Vitamin C:** Found in fruits like oranges and strawberries, and vegetables like bell peppers and kale, vitamin C reduces cortisol levels and boosts the immune system.
- **Omega-3 Fatty Acids:** For vegetarians, sources like flaxseeds, chia seeds, and walnuts are great for lowering inflammation and helping prevent cortisol spikes.
- **Magnesium:** Abundant in spinach, chard, and other leafy greens, magnesium helps regulate cortisol levels and improve sleep quality.

Dietary Plans: Creating meal plans that enhance overall wellness includes:

- **Balanced Meals:** Incorporate a variety of plant-based foods to ensure a range of essential nutrients. Focus on a colorful palette of fruits, vegetables, whole grains, and plant-based proteins.
- **Consistent Eating Times:** Regular meal times help regulate your body's natural cycles and reduce stress.
- **Mindful Eating:** Focus on enjoying each bite and recognizing when you are full to improve your relationship with food.

5. Mental and Emotional Health Practices

Mindfulness Techniques:

- **Daily Meditation:** Even five minutes per day can increase mindfulness, reducing stress.
- **Mindful Breathing:** Focus on deep, even breaths to reduce anxiety.

Stress Management Tools:

- **Breathing Exercises:** Techniques like the 4-7-8 breathing can calm the mind.
- **Guided Imagery:** Visualizing calming images to distract from stressful thoughts.

Building Emotional Resilience:

- **Cognitive Reframing:** Change your perspective on stressful situations to manage your emotional response.
- **Gratitude Journaling:** Regularly noting what you are thankful for can improve your mood and resilience.

6. Integrating Wellness into Daily Life

Routine Building:

- **Establish Routines:** Set specific times for meals, exercise, and relaxation.
- **Small Changes:** Start with manageable changes to build confidence and reduce overwhelm.

Work-Life Balance:

- **Set Boundaries:** Clearly define work hours and personal time to prevent overlap.
- **Prioritize Downtime:** Ensure you schedule time for relaxation and hobbies to recharge.

By incorporating these aspects of physical activity, nutritional wellness, and mental health practices into your daily life, you can build a robust foundation for holistic wellness. This comprehensive approach not only helps in reducing stress but also enhances your overall health and well-being, paving the way for a more balanced and fulfilling life for all, including our vegetarian readers.

Work-Life Balance: Understanding and Implementing Effective Strategies

When we talk about work-life balance, it's important to clarify that it isn't merely about reducing work hours or spending more time at home. True work-life balance involves meaningful engagement in both professional and personal spheres, ensuring that our time in each area is spent effectively and enriches our lives.

Quality Over Quantity in Family Time: Work-life balance does not mean you leave your professional responsibilities unfinished, especially when they demand your attention. It's about managing your professional duties without letting them encroach on the essential personal time that your family deserves. Watching TV at home after leaving the office early doesn't embody work-life balance if you're not mentally present with your loved ones.

The essence of work-life balance is about providing quality attention to your family when they need you. It involves:

- **Engaging Actively:** Whether it's spending half an hour of undistracted time with your spouse or actively listening and responding to your child's questions, the quality of the interaction matters more than the duration. These moments, though brief, should be fulfilling and enriching for both you and your family.

- **Being Present:** True presence means when you're with your family, your focus should be on them. This isn't just physical presence, but emotional and mental engagement too. It's about making sure that the time you spend together is valuable and contributes positively to your relationships.
- **Scheduling Family Time:** Just as you would schedule an important meeting at work, schedule regular intervals dedicated solely to family activities. This ensures that your home life receives the attention and care it deserves and is not left to fit in around your work commitments only.

Balancing Professional Demands: Balancing does not mean neglecting your professional responsibilities. Instead, it's about :

- **Effective Time Management:** Organize your work schedule to maximize efficiency, allowing you to meet professional obligations while preserving dedicated family time. Techniques such as prioritizing tasks, delegating when possible, and setting realistic deadlines can help manage professional workload without compromising personal time.

- **Setting Boundaries:** Communicate clearly with your employer and colleagues about your boundaries. This might include not answering emails or calls during certain hours unless there's an emergency, thus protecting your personal time.
- **Flexibility:** When possible, leverage flexibility in your work arrangements. If your job allows for flexible hours or remote work, use these options to design a workday that accommodates important family activities or needs.

Incorporating these elements into your daily routine supports a sustainable work-life balance that doesn't just benefit your personal life but enhances your professional productivity as well. By being fully present and engaged in both areas, you not only meet your responsibilities but also build stronger, more meaningful connections with those you care about.

Case Studies and Success Stories: Demonstrating Holistic Wellness in Action

The value of holistic wellness strategies is best illustrated through real-life examples. These case studies highlight individuals and organizations that have successfully integrated holistic wellness into their routines, showing tangible benefits in both personal and professional realms.

Case Study 1: The Mindful Tech Company

Background: A mid-sized tech startup recognized that its employees were experiencing high levels of stress due to demanding project deadlines and constant technological disruptions.

Implementation: The company introduced a holistic wellness program that included:

- **Mindfulness Workshops:** Weekly mindfulness sessions were introduced to teach employees techniques to enhance present-moment awareness and reduce stress.
- **Flexible Work Hours:** To better accommodate personal life and reduce burnout, flexible working hours were implemented.
- **Physical Wellness Facilities:** The company provided on-site fitness facilities and subsidized gym memberships to encourage physical activity.

Outcome: After six months, the company reported a 30% decrease in reported stress levels and a noticeable improvement in employee productivity. Employee retention rates improved, and the company culture shifted towards a more supportive and engaged workforce.

Case Study 2: The Healing School

Background: An elementary school in a high-stress urban area noticed a decline in student engagement and an increase in behavioral issues, which were attributed to stress and anxiety among students.

Implementation: The school integrated holistic wellness into its curriculum by:

- **Nutritional Changes:** The school cafeteria introduced a nutrition program focused on balanced, healthy meals that are known to support cognitive function and stabilize energy levels.
- **Yoga Classes:** Incorporating daily yoga sessions for students to help them manage stress and improve physical health.
- **Parental Involvement Workshops:** The school offered workshops for parents on stress management techniques and the importance of maintaining a stress-free environment at home.

Outcome: Students demonstrated improved attention spans, better academic performance, and reduced behavioral problems. Feedback from parents was overwhelmingly positive, noting enhanced family dynamics and better handling of stress at home.

References for Further Reading:

1. **Harvard Business Review:** Articles on how companies integrate wellness programs to boost productivity and employee satisfaction.
2. **Journal of Pediatric Psychology:** Studies detailing the impact of school-based wellness programs on student behavior and academic performance.

These case studies underscore the effectiveness of holistic wellness strategies in various settings. By addressing the physical, mental, and emotional needs of individuals, both organizations were able to foster environments that not only enhance well-being but also promote greater efficiency and harmony. These success stories serve as inspiring examples for others looking to implement similar wellness initiatives in their communities or workplaces.

Challenges and Overcoming Barriers

Adopting a holistic wellness lifestyle can be incredibly rewarding, yet it's not without its challenges. Understanding these obstacles and strategizing ways to overcome them is crucial for sustained success.

Common Obstacles:

- **Time Constraints:** Many people struggle to find time for regular exercise, proper meal preparation, and mental health practices due to busy schedules.
- **Cultural and Social Barriers:** Some wellness practices may not align with cultural norms or social settings, making them harder to adopt.
- **Economic Factors:** Access to healthy food options, fitness facilities, and wellness programs can be limited by economic constraints.
- **Motivation and Discipline:** Maintaining the discipline for regular physical activity, dietary management, and mental health practices requires consistent motivation, which can wane over time.

Strategies for Overcoming These Barriers:

- **Prioritization and Planning:** Treat wellness activities with the same importance as work meetings or family commitments. Schedule them into your calendar to ensure they are not overlooked.

- **Inclusive Approaches:** Adapt wellness practices to fit within cultural and social norms, or find community groups that support these activities.
- **Budget-Friendly Options:** Explore cost-effective options for nutrition and exercise, such as preparing meals at home, using online workout videos, or joining community exercise groups.
- **Build a Support Network:** Engage friends, family, or online communities who share your wellness goals to keep motivation high and maintain accountability.

Future Directions in Holistic Wellness

The field of holistic wellness is ever-evolving, with new trends and technologies shaping how we approach health and stress management.

Emerging Trends:

- **Technology Integration:** Wearable devices and mobile apps are becoming increasingly sophisticated, offering more personalized insights into health metrics and providing tailored wellness recommendations.

- **Mindfulness and Mental Health:** As awareness of mental health's importance grows, more workplaces and schools are integrating mindfulness practices into their daily routines.
- **Nutritional Science Advances:** Continuous advancements in nutritional science lead to better understanding of how specific nutrients affect mental health and stress levels, influencing dietary recommendations.
- **Holistic Health Spaces:** The rise of spaces designed specifically for holistic health, such as wellness hubs that combine fitness, nutrition, and mental health services under one roof, is becoming more common.

Looking Ahead: The Future of Stress Management

Imagine a future where taking care of your whole self is easier and fits naturally into your day. This is where we're headed with holistic wellness—making it not just more reachable for everyone, but also tailored to each person and a normal part of daily life.

As we learn more about how different parts of wellness work together, our ways of managing stress will get even better. These methods will be simpler to keep up with and will help us deeply, making our lives smoother and more peaceful.

By understanding the challenges ahead and keeping up with new trends, we can better handle these challenges and use new chances to improve our wellness routines. This helps us not only to handle stress better but also to thrive in every part of our lives. This exciting future can bring us all more joy and less stress, helping us and future generations to live fuller, healthier lives.

Conclusion

As we conclude this exploration of holistic wellness, we've uncovered the transformative power of integrating physical activity, balanced nutrition, and mental health practices into our daily lives. This isn't just about managing stress—it's about creating a lifestyle that empowers us to thrive.

Remember, the journey to holistic wellness is about making small, consistent changes. Each step forward is a step toward a more vibrant and balanced life. As we move into the next chapter, "Transforming Stress into Success: Turning Challenges into Opportunities," we will build on this foundation, exploring how to turn stress into a catalyst for growth and achievement.

Let's continue to embrace each part of our lives with intention and positivity, turning everyday challenges into stepping stones for success. Join us as we discover how to transform stress into a powerful tool for personal and professional development.

Chapter 7

Transforming Stress into Success: Turning Challenges into Opportunities

"Out of difficulties grow miracles." — Jean de La Bruyère

In this final chapter, we explore the profound concept of transforming stress into success, turning what often feels like a hindrance into a powerful tool for personal and professional growth. Here, we dive into practical methods and inspiring examples that illustrate how reinterpreting challenges can lead not only to overcoming them but also to thriving because of them.

Harnessing Stress for Growth

Stress, when channeled correctly, can become a motivator, a clarifier of priorities, and a sharpener of focus. It can push us to our limits, revealing our latent potentials and opening up paths to achievements we never thought possible. The key is in changing our perspective towards stress, seeing it as an opportunity to test our resilience and adaptability.

Practical Methods for Transformation

1. **Reframing Perspective**: Learn to view stressful situations as challenges rather than threats. This shift in perspective can change how you react, making you more likely to engage positively and find solutions.
2. **Goal Setting**: Use stress as a catalyst to set realistic, clear goals. Stress often highlights what is most important by showing us where our limits and pressures lie.
3. **Stress Inoculation**: Gradually expose yourself to stress in controlled amounts that can help build your tolerance over time. This technique is much like strengthening muscles through exercise.

Inspiring Examples of Success

- **The Entrepreneur**: Consider the story of a startup founder who used the stress of potential failure as a driving force to innovate and adapt his business model. His company not only survived but thrived, expanding into new markets with a robust new approach.
- **The Athlete**: An athlete might use the stress of competition to enhance focus and performance, channeling nervous energy into a powerful drive towards victory.

Encouraging a Positive Outlook on Career Challenges

- **Professional Development**: Embrace stress as a part of your professional growth. Each stressful situation teaches a lesson, whether it's about personal limits, new skills, or unexpected opportunities.
- **Mentorship and Community**: Engage with mentors and a community that views stress as a part of the growth process. Sharing experiences and solutions can reinforce the positive aspects of stress.

Concluding Thoughts: Stress as a Gateway to Success

As we conclude this journey, remember that the transformation of stress into success is not about eliminating stress but about mastering it. By embracing stress as an inevitable part of life and learning to harness its energy, you can not only cope with challenges more effectively but also use them as stepping stones to greater achievements.

This approach doesn't just alleviate stress; it redefines it, turning it into a dynamic force that drives us forward. Let us step into the future with a new outlook on stress, ready to transform every challenge into an opportunity for success.

As we move beyond this book, consider how you can apply these insights in your daily life and career, transforming stress from a shadow into a highlight of your personal and professional journey.

Embarking on a Journey of Self-Discovery: Reflective Questions for Personal Growth

As you turn to the questions in the this section, consider this an invitation to deepen your journey into self-awareness. These inquiries are tools, meant to shine a light on how you navigate stress, interact in your work environment, and grow personally. By approaching these questions with honesty and introspection, you're not just answering queries—you're engaging in a profound exploration of your inner landscape. This process can reveal powerful truths about your patterns and potential. Let this be a moment of quiet reflection where you allow yourself the space to listen deeply to your own wisdom. Embrace this opportunity, for in these answers lies the potential for transformative growth and a more fulfilling life.

1. How often do you feel overwhelmed by your responsibilities at work?
2. Can you identify what triggers your stress most frequently?
3. How do you typically react when you feel overwhelmed at work?
4. Do you have a routine that helps you manage daily stress?

5. How comfortable do you feel asking for help when you're stressed?
6. What physical symptoms of stress have you noticed in yourself?
7. How often do you engage in physical activity to help manage stress?
8. Do you feel like you have a healthy work-life balance?
9. How do you decompress after a stressful day at work?
10. Have you ever felt burnt out? If so, what were the signs?
11. How do you prioritize your tasks when everything feels important?
12. How often do you take breaks during your workday?
13. Do you practice mindfulness or meditation? If so, how often?
14. How connected do you feel to your colleagues on a personal level?
15. How often do you feel irritable or impatient with coworkers?
16. How comfortable are you with saying "no" at work?
17. Do you feel like you can be your true self at work?
18. How often do you feel appreciated by your peers or superiors?

19. Do you think you have a healthy diet that supports your mental health?
20. How much quality sleep do you get on an average night?
21. Do you have any hobbies that help you manage stress?
22. How often do you reflect on your personal and professional growth?
23. Do you set clear and attainable goals for yourself?
24. How do you celebrate your achievements, no matter how small?
25. Are you able to forgive yourself for mistakes and learn from them?
26. How do you handle criticism at work?
27. Do you feel that your work environment is supportive and safe?
28. How often do you feel confident in your professional abilities?
29. Do you feel your work is meaningful and impacts positively?
30. How do you handle conflicts with colleagues?
31. Are you able to disconnect from work during your off hours?
32. How do you manage the pressure of deadlines?
33. Have you ever felt discriminated against or undervalued at work?

34. How often do you experience anxiety about work-related matters?
35. Do you feel that your workplace promotes mental wellness?
36. How often do you engage in deep, meaningful conversations with family or friends?
37. Do you feel you have enough support from your personal relationships?
38. How often do you feel the need to compete with your colleagues?
39. How do you ensure you stay hydrated and nourished during work hours?
40. Do you use any apps or tools to help manage your stress or organize your tasks?
41. How often do you check in with yourself emotionally during the day?
42. Do you feel that you manage stress in a healthy way?
43. What steps have you taken to improve your mental and emotional well-being in the last year?
44. Do you feel that you have a good understanding of what causes stress in your life?
45. How do you approach setting boundaries for personal and professional interactions?
46. What are your strategies for maintaining focus when faced with distractions?

47. How often do you find yourself thinking about work outside of work hours?
48. How proactive are you in seeking feedback on your performance?
49. Do you feel that your contributions at work are recognized and valued?
50. What are your strategies for personal development and continuous learning?

About the Author

Born in a humble village in Rajasthan, India, where modern conveniences such as paved roads and electricity were luxuries that arrived only in his late teens, Umar's journey is a testament to resilience and perseverance. From these modest beginnings, he pursued mechanical engineering and went on to earn a series of prestigious certifications, establishing himself as a recognized expert in his field.

His credentials include:

- NLP Practitioner By Dr YS Rathod
- PMP (Project Management Professional) from the Project Management Institute, USA.
- MICorr (Professional Membership) from the Institute of Corrosion, UK.
- Senior Corrosion Technologist from NACE International, now known as the Association for Materials Protection and Performance (AMPP).
- Authorized Inspector from the National Board of Boiler and Pressure Vessel Inspectors, USA.
- Professional Certificate in Data Science from Harvard.

Each step in Umar's career has been guided by a commitment to learning and excellence, reflecting his deep engagement with both the technical and human aspects of his profession. His unique perspective is enriched by his varied experiences, from the rural life of his youth to his academic and professional achievements on the global stage. This book brings together his profound insights into workplace dynamics, stress management, and holistic wellness, offering readers practical guidance rooted in a lifetime of real-world experiences.

www.ingramcontent.com/pod-product-compliance
Lightning Source LLC
LaVergne TN
LVHW010112170826
845678LV00012B/2362

* 9 7 8 9 3 6 0 8 7 5 4 9 7 *